There's a little
WITCH
in every woman

There's a little WITCH in every woman

MIDIA STAR

WITH CONTRIBUTIONS BY FAOLIN NA AMAROK

BARNES & NOBLE BOOKS
NEW YORK

This edition published by Barnes & Noble,
Inc. by arrangement with Godsfield Press

2004 Barnes & Noble Books

M 10 9 8 7 6 5 4 3 2 1

ISBN 0-7607-4579-X

Disclaimer
This book is intended to give general information
only. The publisher, authors, and distributor
expressly disclaim all liability to any person
arising directly or indirectly from the use of, or
any errors or omissions in, the information given
in this book. The adoption and application of the
information in this book is at readers' discretion
and is their sole responsibility.

Designed and produced by
The Bridgewater Book Company

Project Editor: Sarah Doughty
Illustrator: Trina Dalziel
Designers: Anna Hunter-Downing and
Ana Bjezancevic

Printed and bound in China

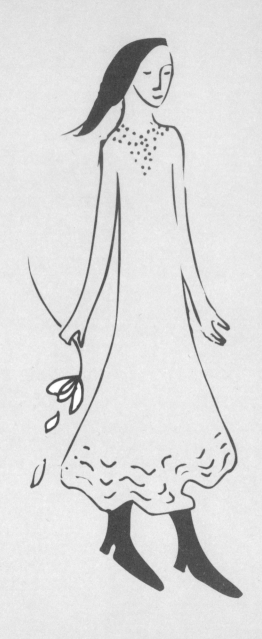

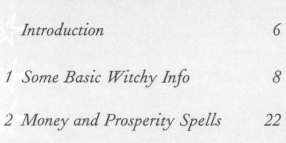

Contents

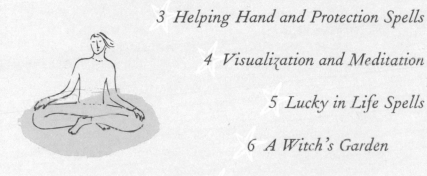

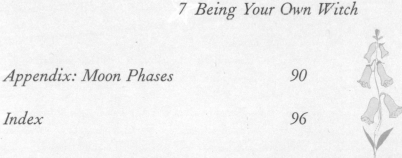

☆ Introduction

The practice of real Magick—we're not talking rabbits and hats here—has been around for thousands of years, and women have always had a natural ability to tap into the unknown, but many of the skills that our great-, great-, great-grandmothers used have been lost over time. Even in today's busy world, every woman, no matter what age, color, or creed, has the ability to enhance her life with a little bit of Magick!

Have you ever knocked on wood for good luck? Thrown spilled salt over your shoulder? Found a four-leaf clover? Or seen a penny and picked it up? All these familiar rituals come from the original believers in Magick—the Celtic Druids. The belief that Magick has anything to do with bat's wings and frog's legs is so far from the truth it's hilarious.

It's never too late to unlock your power and natural ability to perform Magick in your everyday life. Real Magick is about making life easier for yourself and attaining what you want out of life. In these modern times of juggling a career with motherhood, managing a family, a mortgage and generally being Superwoman, we all need a helping hand and that helping hand can be found by applying a little Magick to your life. The great thing is, you don't need to be a full-fledged witch, attend any initiation ceremonies, belong to a coven, or even own a broomstick! Any woman can do it!

Whether you want to improve your marriage, see an increase in your finances, improve your health, or start a new career, *There's a Little Witch in Every Woman* will show you how. With tried and tested spells designed especially for the modern woman, *There's a Little Witch in Every Woman* is the modern woman's magickal helping hand. Release the little witch in you and discover that you have the power to create the life you want! This book is dedicated to the little witch in you!

1 Some Basic Witchy Info

Background Beliefs

Although the art of Magick is accessible to anyone, it's worth bearing in mind some vital witchy information that will help to enhance the power of Magick in your spells…

The Wiccan Rules

Wicca (from the Celtic for "wise") is another word for witchcraft. Its three main rules witches should follow, or ignore at their peril, are:

1 *Do as you wish, so long as it harms no other living creature.*
2 *Do as you wish, so long as you don't interfere with anyone else's free will. (This includes love spells!)*
3 *Whatever you do in life, be it good or bad, returns to you sevenfold.*

In other words, do whatever Magick you want, but never allow it to interfere with or harm another person. The laws of the universe are such that if someone has hurt you, be satisfied that they will be "paid back" in some way, at some point in their lives. Don't be tempted to get revenge. Revenge spells only come back upon you—and seven times as bad at that! This is known as "kick-back." However, it is also worth mentioning here that you cannot do harm by accident.

Belief is Half the Battle

Henry Ford was quoted as saying, "If you think you can, or think you can't, you're right," and this applies as well to the forces of Magick. If you convince yourself that the art of Magick is a load of mumbo jumbo, then no amount of spell craft you do will work for you. The mind is the most powerful and receptive computer in the world and believing in your magickal work will not only improve your chances of gaining what you want out of life, but also will give you faster results. Anyone can mix a few herbs and recite a few mystical words, but unless you open your mind and truly believe that a spell will work, you won't achieve the results you want. Remember, real witchcraft is a helping hand to achieving all you want in life, not a game where you wave a magic wand and everything is handed to you on a plate. Therefore, respect it and believe in it. The belief in The Craft can have extraordinary effects on all aspects of your life. Women who have never used spell work before have said that since doing Magick they have become more confident and have more self-esteem than ever before!

The Influence of the Moon

The moon has a great deal of importance in the art of Magick and the phase of the moon can enhance a spell to optimum performance. Each phase of the moon is considered suitable for a different magickal purpose. The New Moon is a time for ending things and so is suitable for banishing something from your life, such as a bully of a boss, or an unsuitable partner. The Waxing Moon, which is the phase from the day after the New Moon to the day of the Full Moon, is the time for attracting things into your life such as an increase in fortune or a job promotion. The Full Moon is the time for bringing things to completion and the Waning Moon is a time for decreasing things in your life, such as unpleasant gossip about you. See the chart at the end of the book to help you see just what position the moon is in at any given time.

Candles and Days

Many witches use not only the position of the moon when preparing a spell, but also specific days and candles to enhance the power of the spell they are performing. The following is a guide to the days and colored candles that are best suited to performing a specific spell.

SPELLS FOR SPECIFIC DAYS

Monday	Is best for health, money, and home issues.
Tuesday	Is best for energy, protection, and friendship.
Wednesday	Is best for exams, legal matters, communication, and attraction.
Thursday	Is best for increase in luck, property matters, and business.
Friday	Is best for affairs of the heart, friends, and money.
Saturday	Is best for breaking habits and banishing things from your life.
Sunday	Is best for general success, money, health, and confidence.

It is believed that a burning candle of the appropriate color can enhance the power of a spell. The following colors are associated with a specific day of the week and should be used if you want to add that extra bit of power to a spell. If you find it difficult to find the right colored candle, you can substitute any color with white to get the same effect.

DAYS AND CANDLE COLORS

Monday	White or silver
Tuesday	Red
Wednesday	Yellow
Thursday	Blue
Friday	Pink
Saturday	Dark blue, black, or red
Sunday	Gold, orange, or yellow

Although any of the spells in this book will work on any given day, to enhance the spell you can use the above information to help you. Say, for example, you wanted to improve your job prospects. You would use a gold or yellow candle and perform the spell on a Sunday, when the moon was in its Waxing or Full Moon phase. If you wanted to stop someone gossiping about you, you would use a dark blue, red, or black candle, perform the spell on a Saturday, when the moon was New or Waning. This is not entirely necessary for a spell to work, but it will give it greater power.

Please and Thank You

When anyone gives you a gift, you say, "Thank you."
When performing a spell it's only courteous to say, "Please,"
when you make your request and "Thank you," when your wish
is granted. Witches believe in the existence of the God and
Goddess of the universe and it is to them that you give thanks.
Always remember when you begin a spell to say
"Please," and end a spell with "Thank you" and
"So mote it be." This simple sentence represents
closure of your spell. Many witches use oblation after
having carried out a spell. Oblation is a gift of thanks
to the universe such as making a small donation to charity
or planting a new plant in your garden.

It won't take long before you see results from your spells, but don't become complacent about it. Doing spells to impress people, taking the easy way out, or assuming that you are invincible because of your Magick, will only result in loss to you, as will using your powers to control someone or take revenge upon another person. It is always worth remembering that when someone wrongs or hurts you, they will be paid back in some way. This is a natural process called *karma*. No amount of sticking pins in a doll will help you get revenge. You will harm only yourself if you decide to use your Magick to pay someone back. Remember that your misfortune will be sevenfold!

The only time we would encourage you to perform such a spell is when you feel that you need protection from someone who may harm you. Even then we would recommend only a protection spell or a return spell to send the misfortune back to its original source. (See Helping Hand and Protection Spells section.)

Special Witchy Dates

Some days in the year are extra special to witches. All these days are pagan celebrations and have been handed down from generation to generation. Known as sabbats, *these days follow the movement of the Sun throughout the year and are thought to bring the very best fortune and prosperity possible. There are four greater sabbats and four lesser sabbats.*

The Four Greater Sabbats

Samhain

Pronounced "sow-in," this sabbat begins on October 31. Otherwise known as the Witches' New Year and also known as Halloween, Samhain is an ideal time for prosperity and for making a new start.

Imbolc

Pronounced "em-bowl/g," this sabbat begins on February 2 and is an ideal time for growth, cleansing, and candle spells.

Beltaine ·

Pronounced "beel-teen," this sabbat begins on May 1 and is traditionally a time for new ideas and sexuality.

Lughnasadh

Pronounced "loo-nass-ad," this sabbat begins on August 1 and is a time to harvest new ideas.

The Four Lesser Sabbats

Winter Solstice

This sabbat begins on December 21 and is a time to take stock of things and plan long term for the future.

Spring Equinox

This sabbat begins on March 21 and is a time for completely changing your life and forgetting the past.

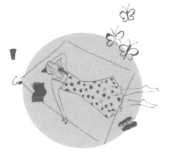

Summer Solstice

This sabbat falls on June 21 and is a time when you should bless your Magick and thank all that it brings you.

Autumn Equinox

This sabbat falls on September 21 and is a time for turning the tides of fortune in your life and for balancing life's commitments.

These dates are especially important to pagans and witches who, if in a coven or group, will hold a celebration festival in honor of the sabbat. For those who wish to work alone (solitary witches) it is a time that will lend extra power to performing a spell.

☆ The Myths

If you're over thirty, you'll remember the witch Samantha from the series Bewitched. *If you're younger, you'll have seen* Sabrina the Teenage Witch, *a 16-year-old who lives with aunts who are witches. Either way, these portrayals of modern witches are in fact false and simply a means of attracting an audience and enhancing viewer ratings. They also annoy us witches!*

Real witches cannot make someone disappear by simply twitching their nose. Nor can they point a finger, wand, or any other implement, say a few rhyming words and make their dreams come true. Witches don't ride broomsticks or vacuum cleaners (even on Halloween), and they don't always wear a little black number, complete with a pointy hat.

In fact, you could have easily been standing next to a modern-day witch today. Most modern witches don't advertise the fact that they can do Magick. They are ordinary women, just like you. They work to pay the bills, just like you, eat the same type of food, and have the same problems juggling modern life. Just as you wouldn't know if you were sitting next to a Christian, a Buddhist, or an atheist, you would have no idea that your work colleague, friend, aunt, or neighbor practiced Magick in their spare time.

The belief that witches are to be feared arose in the times when the Christian Church wanted to recruit more believers. Anyone who held a different belief was persecuted, including followers of the pagan religion of Wicca. But witches have never done and will never do anything that harms another living thing. We believe that all living things should be cherished and we are very much in tune with nature. We believe that everyone, regardless of faith, color, or creed, should be able to live their life as they wish without fear or persecution from others. Witchcraft is about helping yourself and others by using your natural magickal gift.

A BOOK OF SHADOWS

A Book of Shadows is basically a book of spells. You can make your own very easily. Most witches keep a Book of Shadows so that they can refer to a particular spell they have successfully used before. Any notebook or exercise book will do, but you might want to buy a special hard-backed book, because this book is going to hold all your magickal notes, to which you will refer time and time again. Many New Age shops sell leather-bound books specifically for use as a Book of Shadows.

When you find a spell that you like and, more importantly, one that works for you, write down all the details in your Book of Shadows. The Internet has many sites about witchcraft and spells and there are many books available with spells for you to try out. As you get more experienced you may want to design your own spells—we will explain more about this at the end of the book. Again, you can write down all your details in your Book of Shadows for future reference. This book is your individual book and should reflect your own unique personality, so make it as pretty, outrageous, or funky as you like. Have fun creating your unique book, which will soon be full of a wealth of information!

Gods and Goddesses

*Witches worship several gods and goddesses, and many witches
will choose one particular "mentor" to help when focusing on
a particular spell. These are just a few we recommend:*

Anubis

Anubis looks like a black Pharaoh hound. He is the finder of lost things
and the protector of the traveler. In modern witchcraft we call upon
Anubis to give us guidance when traveling or on vacation, or for help in
finding something lost.

Hathor

Hathor is the cow goddess and represents beauty and love. She is the
patron of women and is called upon to bring harmony and love into
our lives.

Isis

Isis is the "mother" goddess. She is the protector of children and mistress
of Magick. A very powerful lady, Isis is called upon when we need help
and protection in any family matters.

Sekhmet

This is a very powerful protector and she is often referred to as the
Lioness. She rules healing, especially after surgery, and can be called
upon for strength in difficult situations or where extra protection
is needed.

When you feel in need of extra help, imagine you are talking to one of
the gods or goddesses and describe the help you need.

Silence is Golden!

Not everyone you come across is going to approve of your new hobby,
and the quickest way to extinguish the power of a spell is to shout about
it from the rooftops. Some people won't understand what witchcraft is
all about. So, while we are not saying that you should hide your spell
crafting activities or be ashamed about practicing The Craft, you should
be aware that not everyone will accept it. Would it be entirely fair to
your children if you suddenly turned up at the school playground
wearing a pointy hat and announced that you were a witch? What if they
told their friends? How would you feel if they were bullied because of
it? Keep your own counsel! It is far more satisfying and exciting to
know that the reason you got a new job, new car, or more money
was due to bringing your natural powers to the fore, rather than
boasting to one and all that you practice Magick. Be warned that
it won't do you any favors! It will simply ruin all the work you have
done. If you think that a friend would benefit from a bit of
witchcraft in her life, you can apply any of the spells in this book
to help anyone in need. Another point to make is that once you
begin to see the changes in your life, you might be tempted to
charge other people for doing spells for them. Please don't! It may
well earn you extra money at the time, but it isn't an acceptable
practice. Don't tell everyone that you can make their lives better by
doing a spell for them—it never works! Consider the consequences you
could cause. As you will see, Magick is a very powerful tool and one not
to be played with. You might just end up making trouble for someone
else. If you really want to help someone, do one of the Helping Hand
and Protection spells without telling them. You will gain as much
satisfaction from simply knowing that you helped.

Now that we've covered some information, we are ready for the fun
part—the spells! It's time to free the little witch in you!

2 Money and Prosperity Spells

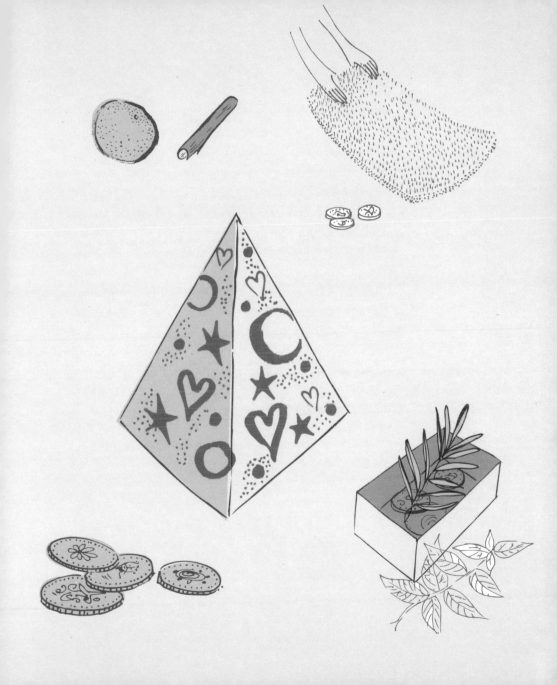

☆ *Introduction*

There are times when we all need a little extra cash in our lives. Spells will work effectively only if there is a genuine need, so don't be greedy! Yes, we would all love to win the lottery, but please think carefully about the genuine need. This doesn't mean that you can't ask for that new cookware or the new computer you want. If it is going to save you time or make you feel more fulfilled and happy, then by all means go for it. If you feel that some extra money would allow you to leave work and spend more time with the kids, or develop your own interests, that's OK, too. If, however, you expect that by doing one of these spells you will never have to work again, be assured that it won't happen. Magick just doesn't work that way.

As mentioned earlier, what we believe is what actually happens in our lives. If we have grown up with the belief that there is never enough money to go around, then that is what we expect from life and that's how our life will turn out. Only when we believe that we deserve better and that our financial needs will be met, will they actually be met. So, although you should not be greedy about becoming wealthy, the more you believe you deserve financial gain, the more power your spell will have.

TIPS AND TALES

* * * * * * * * * *

There are many tales and superstitions about gaining money and prosperity. These are a few of our favorites!

To protect your home at all times, sprinkle a trail of salt along the front door. Leave it for up to one week and then vacuum it up and replace it with new salt.

*

To always have enough money in your household, place three silver coins under your doormat.

*

At the stroke of midnight on New Year's Eve, open your front door to welcome the New Year in and open the back door to let the Old Year out.

*

For protection when you are going out, draw an imaginary circle around you and say "Goddess within, Goddess without, make a circle all about. Keep good in and evil out, Goddess within and Goddess without."

*

To attract prosperity to your house use a cinnamon and orange air freshener in your house.

A Money Maker Pyramid

This spell is ideal if you want to see an increase in your general fortune. Maybe you want some money to buy a specific item, or perhaps you need money for a vacation. For centuries pyramids have held a mystical power. Try this simple spell and see how easy it is to attract money into your life.

INGREDIENTS

* * * * * * *

A sheet of 8 ½" x 11" (21 cm x 28 cm) paper, in your favorite color

Clear adhesive tape

Some shiny stickers (the kind kids use)

A pen, ruler, and scissors

A few silver or gold coins

Draw three triangles of the same size on the paper and cut out the three shapes. Write "My Money Magnet" on each of the three shapes and decorate each with your shiny stickers. Make it as attractive as possible and as fun as you like.

Using the adhesive tape, tape all three shapes together to form a pyramid. It doesn't matter if you are not creative, or if it looks a bit out of shape; the main thing is that it is your own design. When you are done, take your pyramid to a room in your house that you enjoy being in—this might be your bedroom or family room. Take some time to look at your model and believe that your pyramid is going to attract money to you. Place your pyramid in the corner of your room with a few of the gold or silver coins under it. If you don't have any coins, make some out of paper. Say:

"Oh Money Lord, look my way, bring me prosperity from this day, with no harm to me or mine. Thank you. So mote it be."

Refresh your pyramid weekly by replacing the coins. Every time you go into the room where your pyramid is, take a moment to look at it and thank it. You will soon see more money coming into your house.

SUCCESS USING THIS SPELL

* * * * * * * * * *

I have used this spell successfully on several occasions; the most recent resulted in the payment of a big commission for some feature writing.

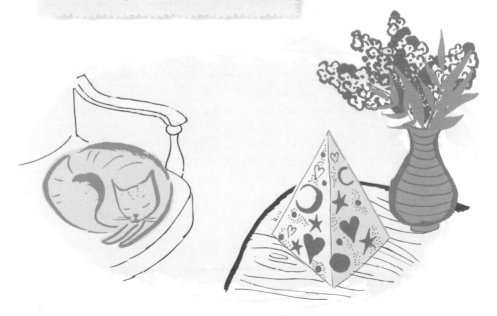

☆ A Money Shaker

Whether you are a working mother, a career woman, or a homemaker, there are times when the finances don't quite stretch far enough, or bills turn up unexpectedly. This fun spell was created by my daughter and makes an excellent birthday or Christmas gift for someone who needs a little Magick in her financial life.

INGREDIENTS

* * * * * * *

A few coins of any denomination

A small box (e.g., a matchbox)

Fresh peppermint and rosemary

Adhesive tape and glue

Decorative paper

Glitter, ribbons, stars

Place a few coins of any denomination into a small box (a matchbox will do), with the peppermint and rosemary (these herbs are available in supermarkets).

Close the box and seal it with adhesive tape. Cut a piece of decorative paper to cover the whole box and glue it onto the box. Next, make it as pretty as you can with glitter, ribbons, stars, and so on. Spend some time focusing on this box and how it is going to bring money into your life.

The idea behind this spell is that when you require a certain amount of cash (be realistic here!) you hold the box in your left hand and visualize for a moment the amount of money you need. Give the box a little shake and say:

"Money, money, come to me. I need (the amount you need), as you can see. Help me till my wish has come, and let my quest harm no one. Thank you. So mote it be."

You will notice that when we say a spell, we always ask that it harm no one. This is purely a precautionary note, but a wise one to use.

Money sometimes comes into people's lives due to someone's misfortune, such as an inheritance, but you shouldn't want anyone to be harmed in your quest for extra money. Please remember to mention this in your spell work.

Carry your money shaker in your purse or handbag, so that it is easily accessible whenever you need it, but please don't abuse it. It will work only when you truly need extra help. Don't lend your money shaker to anyone. If you think a friend could do with some extra cash, show her how to make one for herself.

Spell provided by Rebecca.

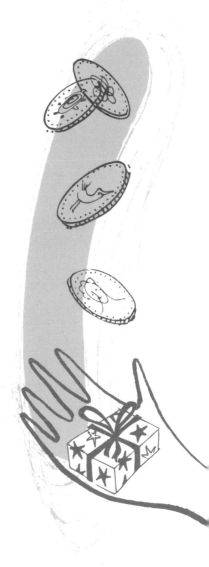

SUCCESS USING THIS SPELL

* * * * * * * * *

Unbeknownst to me, my daughter invented this spell for extra pocket money and succeeded in getting an increase in her allowance. I have my own money shaker, which has worked every time I've used it, for everything from needing the money for school lunches to helping me purchase my new PC for work!

☆ Dream Board Spell

In the busy lives we lead, it's all too easy to forget about our own wants and needs. Women have always put their partners' and children's needs before their own and have ended up feeling as though the dreams they once had have become lost in the big wide world. What happened to those goals we once had? They got left behind in the maternity ward, that's what!

INGREDIENTS

* * * * * * * *

A large piece of white cardboard

⟪⟪

An illustration of your dreams
(these can be your own drawings,
magazine cutouts, etc.)

⟪⟪

Some colored pens
(borrow the kids')

⟪⟪

Some glitter

⟪⟪

A favorite photograph of yourself

⟪⟪

Some glue

Women are told by society that they can't have it all. They can't have both a family and a career. And you know what? They believe it. Remember what we said about believing—it comes true! In fact, it is possible to retrieve those dreams you once had of being financially independent, affording that new car, or getting that promotion and still being able to maintain a secure and loving home life. We're going to show you just how to do it…

You're going to get creative now! It doesn't matter if you're not naturally artistic; the important thing is that you create your Dream Board. Glue the photo of yourself at the bottom right-hand corner of the page. Be sure to use one of your favorite photos. Next, draw a big "thinking bubble" covering the entire page, so that it looks like you are thinking about what you want. Draw or cut out pictures of things that you want in your life. Your dreams, material wants and needs, and your goals. Maybe you've always wanted to be a rock star and learn to play the guitar. If so, get

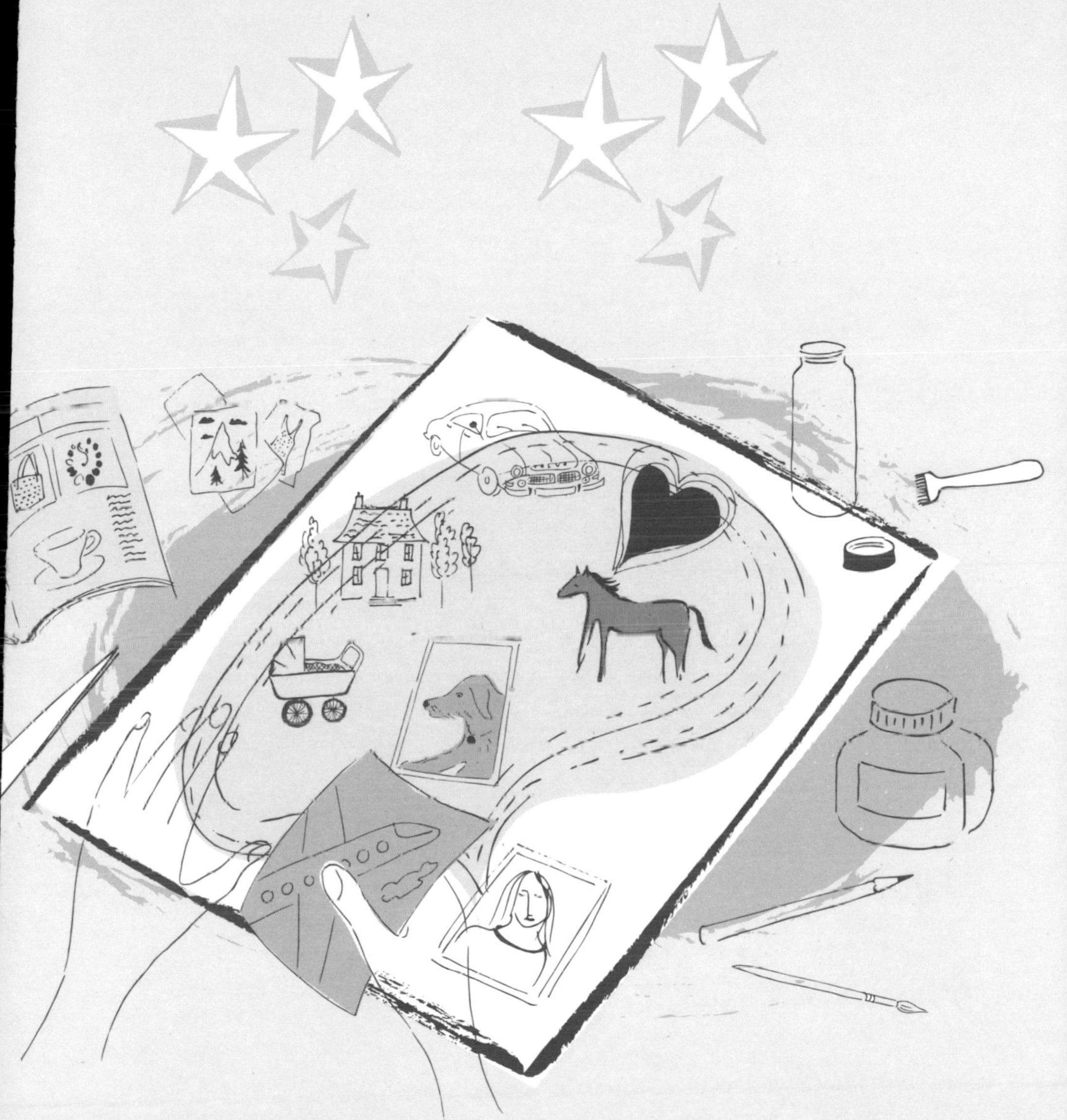

a picture of the guitar you want or a picture of a female guitarist you want to be like. Who cares if you're 55? Maybe you want to lose five pounds (about 2 kg) and have a new wardrobe. If this is the case, find a picture of someone whom you admire, or of the clothes you would like to buy. Whatever it is you want, stick it in your thinking bubble! If you are looking for a new job, see if you can get a letterhead from the company you are interested in working for and stick that in the bubble. Under each picture add a small caption, such as: "I am the head chef at this smart restaurant," or "I can play guitar and am forming a band." Always put it in the present tense—the mind and the universe are more receptive to "now."

When you have filled up your thinking bubble, take time to look at each dream. Make sure that you are doing it for yourself and not for someone else. Outside of the "bubble" write in glitter, "Maybe not today, maybe not tomorrow, but my dreams WILL come true."

Pin this board onto your wall, fridge, back of the door, or wherever you will see it every day. Try to take ten minutes each day to look over your Dream Board and consider how you are going to attain your dreams. If it's possible for someone to have won the lottery last week, then it's possible for you to win, too! If someone you admire has made a success of her life, then it's possible for you to be like that, too!

Recall Henry Ford's comment, "If you think you can, or if you think you can't—you're right." If you find yourself looking at your Dream Board and thinking, "That's all very well, but I'll never become a doctor" (or whatever your dream is), then you won't. If your dream is to get out of an abusive relationship, but every time you look at your Dream Board and think that you will never do it, then you never will escape. You need to believe that, even though life may look grim now, YOU have the power to change it. The only hard part is believing that you have the power!

Another idea for this spell is to find pictures illustrating each of your dreams and placing each one in a small silver photo frame. These not only look nice on your wall, but will also remind you of your dreams all the time. If, for example, one of your dreams is to buy a new house, visit a real estate agent and find your perfect house. Ask for a detailed description, including a photograph of your dream house and place the photo in your frame. If you want to lose weight, find a picture of someone at your target weight. Cut it out and place it in your frame. This alternative to the Dream Board is ideal if you don't want anyone else to know what you are up to. All others will see is a series of photos.

A great additional technique for speeding up this spell (and all the spells in this book) is visualization. We have included another section on this subject because it is so important to spell work. Please read this section whenever doubt sets in!

Spell provided by Midia Star.

SUCCESS USING THIS SPELL

* * * * * * * * * *

I have used the Dream Board spell to great success. One time I was living in an awful apartment and our landlord had suddenly announced that he intended to sell the house. I spent months focusing on my Dream Board, which illustrated a design of a house that I wanted to live in, in my home village. The house didn't exist at that time, but within eight months I was offered a great deal on a house that looked just like my drawing!

A New Moon Money Bowl

There is and always will be enough money available in the universe, but we often limit ourselves without even noticing it. As mentioned before, if we have been brought up believing that we will only ever have a certain amount of money, then this is as far as we will get in life. If we open our minds to the fact that all our financial needs can be met with plenty left over, then we will attract new opportunities in our lives that we may well have overlooked before. I have used this money magnet spell time and time again with great success.

INGREDIENTS

* * * * * * *

A glass bowl

Filtered water

Three gold floating candles

Some flower petals

A few silver coins

A jelly jar

Take the glass bowl and fill it with the filtered water. Place the three gold candles and the petals on top of the water. Light the candles and then throw the silver coins into the bowl. Concentrate and ask the goddess to help you bring money in. Visualize more money coming into your home. When you feel ready, go outside and say, "Thank you," to the goddess and bow three times. Leave the candles to burn down safely. (Do not leave candles burning if you have to leave the room!) Dry the coins, place them in the jelly jar, and place the jar on a sunny windowsill. Add silver coins to the jar when you can. When you have a few more coins in your jar, you should place three of them under your doormat, so that every visitor brings money with them. You can also place three of your coins in a compartment in your purse. This will attract money to your purse. If you don't have any real coins, you could make some out of foil.

SUCCESS USING THIS SPELL

* * * * * * * * * *

I have used this spell many times and each time it has attracted the money I have needed. The most important aspect of this spell is the visualization. Don't ask for more than you actually need, or it won't work for you!

Spell provided by Faolin Na Amarok.

Wishing Well Spell

Herbs have always played an important part in witchcraft and this is a wonderful old spell designed for the use of herbs that are easily accessible and can be found in your garden or at the local supermarket. It is widely believed that different herbs should be used for different spells, but if you don't have the required herb available, you can always use mixed herbs.

INGREDIENTS

* * * * * * *

Certain herbs are best used for particular types of spells:

Bay for success wishes

Rosemary for promotion wishes

Verbena for general wishes

Peppermint for prosperity and money wishes

The Wishing Well Spell is very simple and should be conducted outside if possible. Look at the ingredients list and decide which category your wish falls under. If it is for more money, for example, you would use peppermint. If, on the other hand, you want to stop a coworker from bullying you, then you would use verbena for general wishes. If you have it available, pour a little glitter into your hand, too.

Next pour a handful of your chosen herb into your left hand and go outside to a spot in the garden where you feel peaceful. Think carefully about what you want from this wish and visualize the end result. For example, if you want to start a new business, see yourself doing just that. See yourself in your new premises. Get excited at the thought of traveling to work to do a job that you love. It's your own business—get excited about that! Think carefully about what you wish for, because wishes *do* come true!

Once you feel ready and satisfied, gently blow your wish into the herbs in your hand. Don't blow too hard or you will blow the herbs away!

Now for the fun part! Imagine that you are standing at the top of a wishing well. Hold your cupped hands above your head and say:

"This is my wish for my wishing well. This is my secret, I shall not tell. Wishes come true, this I believe; with your help, my wish will come true for me."

Now throw the herbs and glitter up into the air and imagine them falling down into your wishing well. Smile to yourself at the thought of your wishing well spell working, then walk away.

Spell provided by Midia Star.

3 Helping Hand and Protection Spells

☆ *Introduction*

Everyone needs a helping hand at some point in their life and there's nothing better than knowing that you have helped a person in need with a little bit of Magick! We may need help, for example, when a friend is in trouble, or ill, or when Mr. Right turns out to be Mr. Not-So-Right-After-All! Remember when doing a helping spell that you should focus on the person you are trying to help. Remember to keep it to yourself. Just be happy to know that you played your little part to help your friend. Magick is not an alternative to medicine, so please do not be under any illusion that you can perform miracles with your Magick. If someone is seriously ill, you must always seek and follow medical advice.

The other spells in this section are for when you feel you need protection in your life. It may be that you get an uneasy feeling about someone or something—remember, you're usually right. If you feel this at any time, use one of the protection spells in this chapter. Often when we are entering unknown circumstances or unknown territory we feel nervous about what is going to happen. Use one of these spells to ask for help and protection. You'll never leave home without one again!

TIPS AND TALES

* * * * * * * * * * * *

Here are a few ideas for giving yourself a helping hand:

Wish upon a solar eclipse to banish something from your life.
Concentrate on a person or situation you want to banish and repeat
nine times, until the sun is in full view again.

*

Carry an acorn in your pocket for endless luck.

*

For a wish to come true, wish upon the very first star that you see
in the sky at night and speak your wish seven times.

*

Catch a leaf as it falls and make a wish.
Picking one up from the ground doesn't count!

The Boiled Egg Spell

*When we are ill our body's natural immune system takes
a battering. This is why it can often take a long time to recover.
Eggs have always symbolized the rebirth of something and
are an excellent tool for use in the Magick of healing.
The following spell is designed to be carried out if someone
you know is suffering from a minor illness such as a cold.*

INGREDIENTS

* * * * * * *

A black felt-tip pen

))⦗⦗(

A hard-boiled egg

When performing a healing spell for someone, it is
important to protect yourself first! Create a circle of
salt around you before doing the spell. If you don't
protect yourself, the person's illness will "jump" from
them to you! If the person is present, roll the egg
across their forehead. If not, think about the person
and how they are feeling right now. Imagine the egg
absorbing the person's illness. Now draw an image on
the egg of the person you are trying to help and write
the person's name above the picture. Say:

"Oh Lady and Lord, release (name of person) *from this
illness that makes him/her suffer so. Thank you. So mote
it be."*

Next kiss the egg and take it to the nearest place
where water is flowing—a stream or a river. Throw
the egg into the body of flowing water and wave
goodbye to the illness. Your friend should soon be
feeling much better.

Spell provided by Midia Star.

To Return a Curse ☆

Have you ever felt that things are against you? There are times when, no matter what you do, nothing seems to go right. There is often a good explanation for this—and we're not talking about voodoo dolls or gypsy curses. Curses can be placed upon you without you knowing about it. It can often be as simple as someone somewhere thinking negative thoughts about you. These thoughts enter the universe and eventually affect your life. It could be that a boss or colleague is intentionally making your working life hell, or someone is spreading malicious gossip about you. Maybe your son or daughter is being bullied at school. If you ever feel that someone is trying to hurt you in this way, this spell will return the curse to its source. Ensure you know for certain who has cursed you—to guess can be dangerous.

Hold the mirror in your hand and say:

"Mighty Hathor, return this curse to (name of the person harming you). *May Hathor be my messenger, as you were for Ra!"*

This spell will take three hours, three days, or three weeks to work. Never perform this spell for fun, or revenge. It won't work and it will be you who will suffer in the end. The idea of this spell is to stop someone deliberately hurting you by reflecting his or her power, not to harm that person.

Spell provided by Faolin Na Amarok.

INGREDIENT

* * * * * * *

A small mirror

☆ Chase the Gremlin!

*There are times in everyone's life when things just don't go right.
The children get sick, the car breaks down, work is a constant
battle, and you seem to have no end of bad luck. Have you ever
considered that a gremlin might be in your house? Sounds like
something out of* The Hobbit, *doesn't it? But it's not as crazy as
you think. Often "spirits" who have passed over don't quite reach
their destination point and are left in a kind of in-between
world—not quite here, but not quite there, either. These little
gremlins, as I like to call them, can cause all sorts of havoc in
this world. If you feel like things just aren't going right, try this
little cleansing spell—it's great fun to do with the kids, too!*

INGREDIENTS

* * * * * * *

*A broom for each person
performing the spell*

⟪⟪

Lots of enthusiasm

You first need to wake up the gremlin in your house!
To do this, take your broom, go to every corner of
your house, and pretend to sweep all the corners out
into the middle of the room. Act as though there are
a bunch of little gremlins huddled together, fast
asleep in each corner. Go on, wake them up! Push
them into the middle of the room. Now go on to the
next room and do the same until all the rooms have
been "swept."

Now you need to go to the last room you
finished sweeping and imagine that you are sweeping
the gremlins out and down the stairs. Do this to all of
the rooms upstairs. Continue until you have swept all
the gremlins into the middle of your living room.
Stand in the center of the room with your broom
and say:

"I'm sure you are very nice, but you don't belong here. I banish you from entering my home again and let you go on your way to your rightful home. Goodbye and blessed be."

Open the front door and sweep all the gremlins outside. If nobody's looking, wave goodbye to those gremlins. You will soon see a big improvement in your life!

Spell provided by Midia Star.

A Spell to Keep Your Cat Safe

Not all witches have cats. Some have dogs, some have hamsters, and some have been known to have more exotic animals such as snakes! Anyone who owns a dog or a cat knows about the cat who stares at empty air, or the dog who growls and refuses to enter a room. Animals have a sixth sense, which they often use to tell us something. Have you ever noticed how your pets react when you are sad or upset? They know instinctively when something is wrong. They know when you are happy or sad and need protection as well as your human friends. Animals can't protect themselves against some of the modern dangers that they are faced with. The following spells are designed to protect your pets and keep them safe.

Take the 13 leaves and crush them with a silver spoon. Mix the leaves with a little chicken or duck fat. Next, place your cat on the table and offer it some of the cream or fish. Say three times:

"Grimalkin, Grimalkin, feasted in my kitchen, where thou shalt stay and never want to stray."

Stroke your cat three times and, as you do so, collect any loose fur and put it in a safe place. Put a little of the mixture you made up on its paws and then let it go outside. Next, take the fur you collected and write on a piece of paper the words that you said above. Wrap the fur in the paper, seal it, and then hide it somewhere. Your cat will be protected.

INGREDIENTS

* * * * * * *

13 leaves of catnip

Some chicken or duck fat

Some cream or fish

A Spell for Other Animals

A simple protection spell for other animals is to visualize golden or blue light surrounding them. Keep the image for as long as possible. Repeat this process once a week to renew it and your pets will be protected from harm.

Spells provided by Faolin Na Amarok

☆ *Fun Housework Spell!*

This is one of my favorite spells! Unfortunately, along with holding down a job, picking up the kids from school, attending PTA meetings, stocking the fridge, providing a taxi service, and maintaining a loving relationship with our partners, women are also expected to keep the house clean and tidy! Whoever thought being a modern woman was easy, thought wrong! However, help is at hand with our Fun Housework Spell. Housework will never be the same again!

INGREDIENTS

* * * * * * *

Filtered or boiled water

Salt

Trash can liners

Music

Lavender oil

An onion

Unfortunately, homes do not yet clean themselves, but with a little bit of Magick, you will soon have your home looking and feeling sparkling clean. You need to pick one day of the week when you are not working and can have a few hours to yourself. A clutter-free home equals a clutter-free life and, if you are practicing Magick, it is essential to have a clean environment to work in.

Start by putting on your favorite music—loud! This will get you in the mood for tackling that clutter. Pick one room at a time and throw out all the clutter that has been building up. Yes, the children's pictures on the fridge may well look homey, but if they've been up for weeks on end, they will have become tired looking. Put them away somewhere and ask the children to make new ones! The magazines and newspapers that have been collecting cobwebs under the coffee table need to be thrown out. The money-off coupons can go—they're probably outdated anyway. If you find items that you think you might

use at a later date, put them all in one big plastic box and store it somewhere.

Once you have rid the house of the weekly clutter, boil some water or buy a few bottles of filtered water, and fill a bucket with the water and add a few drops of lavender oil. Next, wash every washable surface—kitchen countertops, wooden floors, doors—everything, from top to bottom. With the music blaring, you'll soon be enjoying the housework!

When you've finally cleared all the clutter and cleaned the house from top to bottom, take your salt and pour it into a bowl. Bless the salt by saying three times:

"This salt I bless to perform and protect."

Pour a trail of salt along the outside of your front door and inside your hallway, and do the same if you have a back door. Next pour a little salt onto each windowsill in your house. This will protect your house and all who live in it. Finally, cut the onion into four equal pieces and hide them in the four corners of the lower rooms in your house. The onion will absorb all negative energy that enters the house.

Spell provided by Midia Star.

☆ To Protect Your Home

We all like to feel safe in our own home. After all, if we can't feel safe there, where can we feel safe? This little spell will ensure your home is protected at all times.

INGREDIENTS

* * * * * * *

*Some sea salt
(available in most supermarkets)*

))))«

Several tea-light candles

Walk around the indoor perimeter of your home. As you do, sprinkle the salt around the house and say:

"Spirits who dwell here, protect this sacred space. Let my door and heart be ever open to the goddess and sealed from misfortune, illness, and unhappiness!"

Light a tea-light candle in each room and say:

"Spirits who dwell here, this gift of light and warmth I give thee, in return for thy blessing. So mote it be."

Your home will now be protected.

✳

Spell provided by Faolin Na Amarok.

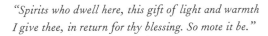

To Protect Your Garden ☆

*This spell is similar to the previous one, but is designed
to protect your garden. Take a day out to devote to your home
and garden and do both protection spells.*

Walk around the perimeter of your garden three times, saying each time:

*"Spirits of nature, protect this sacred space, bless the earth I tread upon.
Let peace and beauty abide in this garden."*

Plant your rose bush and say:

*"Spirits of nature, this gift I give thee in return for thy blessing.
So mote it be."*

This simple ritual will keep your
garden protected.

Spell provided by Faolin Na Amarok.

4 Visualization and Meditation

Become a Child Again!

Meditation and visualization play an important part in spell-craft work. If you have young children, it's worth studying them. Why? Because visualization is a natural part of their lives. At Christmas children are always asked, "What is Santa going to bring you?" The reply is always whatever gifts they want. They don't worry where the money comes from to buy these gifts. They simply assume they are going to get them—end of story. And the result is that they do often get these gifts.

It's only when we get older that we lose this natural power to get what we want. Why? Because instead of believing that we will reach our goals and dreams, we start to doubt them and think that we can't achieve them. We believe that we won't have much money for Christmas and that we could never be clever enough to go to medical school. What we think quickly becomes reality!

As soon as you let doubt in, you might just as well give up and go home. So why do we do this? The answer is because this is how we are brought up. If everyone in the world shared a positive attitude, we would all achieve our childhood dreams. Whatever your dream or goal is, believe that it is going to happen. If you do this, you will get there. It may take months, even years, but you will get there in the end.

Role Models ☆

*We all have role models we look up to. They may be fictional
heroes or real people, it doesn't matter. What does matter is the
fact that if Sandra Bullock can become an award-winning actress,
then so can you. If Danielle Steele can spend her days writing
best-selling novels, instead of working 40 hours a week at the
local supermarket, then you can, too. If the doctor you saw last
week can go to medical school for five years and qualify, then
what's stopping you from doing it?*

Anything is possible and, if we have a role model, or someone
we can look up to and say,

"Yes, that's what I want to be like,"

then so much the better. Whatever your
dream is, there is bound to be someone
out there who is living that dream.
Find out as much as you can about
that person. How did she get her
big break? How did she cope with
returning to school?

    Cut out pictures of your role
model and stick them on your
Dream Board or in your Book of
Shadows. This simple exercise will
keep reminding you that it is possible
to get to where you want to be. If it
wasn't, then there wouldn't be another
person already living that dream.

Fake it Until You Make it!

The biggest part of making your dreams come true is to really believe that you are that new person, living out your dream. Women especially don't like to sing their own praises—how often have you heard, "Oh, I'm just a housewife,"? If you convince people that this is all you are, you not only believe that this is all you amount to, you're telling them that you don't think very highly of yourself.

Let's look at an example: Say you're a woman who stays at home looking after the children, but would love to train as a teacher. You might say to people *"Oh, I am just a housewife,"* but if you want this dream to become a reality, you could say,

"When the children have started school I am going to become a teacher."

Doesn't this sound better to you? If your dream is to be financially independent, then stop worrying how the gas bill is going to get paid and start living like you are a millionaire. You don't have to be a millionaire to look or act like one. Believe that you are rich. Even if you can't afford that luxury vacation home in the Bahamas, convince yourself that you can! It's a great pretending game. Just like when you were a child and pretended that you were a princess. You convinced yourself that you wore beautiful princess clothes, and the saucepan on your head was the most beautiful crown there could ever be!

When you start believing that you are living your dream, you send out invisible signals. You radiate confidence, which in turn brings you into contact with new people and new opportunities. When you convince yourself that you are this person living your ideal life, you will convince other people. New opportunities will come your way.

Dream Your Dream

A great exercise is to visualize that you are already the person you want to be and to write it down in a few paragraphs as if you were answering someone's question. Say you presently work in an office, but it has always been your dream to run your own New Age business, lose a few pounds (kilos), have a partner who treats you like a princess, and be financially independent.

You would write something like this:

My life is perfect! I am now down to my ideal weight. I quit my office job a year ago and opened up my own New Age store called "New Living." The store is a great success and makes me financially independent, so that I no longer have to worry about paying my bills. My partner is warm, kind, and loving and treats me like a princess.

You could add more; it's up to you. The idea is that you can really see your future life. Throw yourself into the future and imagine, if you didn't have to worry about money, or anything else, how you would like to be. We're not on this planet that long. Wouldn't it be better to be living out your dreams, instead of just existing?

If, during this exercise, you find that you can't really visualize yourself performing a major operation (or whatever your goal might be) then think carefully about it. Is this really your dream, or is it someone else's dream? It might be that you don't really want to be a surgeon, but your father wanted you to be one, and you actually want to join the circus!

The way you will know if it's your dream or someone else's is if you get an excited feeling when you write about your ideal life. If you do, then it's your dream life. If you don't, then you might be living your life for someone else.

☆ *Visualization and Spells*

Most spells require you to visualize the outcome. Magick is mind power and the stronger it is, the more productive it will be. Doubt is your worst enemy. Belief and faith in what you are doing can move mountains. Some spells, such as candle spells, don't require visualization because you are already tapping into the higher power. You need to focus on just the subject at hand. Try to push the thoughts of whether to give the kids fish sticks for dinner out of your mind and really concentrate on your goals, dreams, and the spell that you are performing.

If you don't visualize the end result of a spell or believe that you will get the result you desire, no spells you do will ever work. If you do spells just for fun, or to see if they really work—they won't! You need to be serious about crafting spells.

☆ *Meditation*

We know exactly what you're thinking! When do I have time to meditate? I'm taking the kids to school, working eight hours a day, washing enough clothes for an army, and trying to visualize! We know, we know! It is hard to find any time for yourself, let alone for regular meditation. However, you will feel so much better if you can just allow yourself ten minutes a day to completely relax and meditate.

Learning to meditate is not difficult. Simply find a quiet time during the day or evening when you will not be disturbed. Sit in a comfortable armchair or lie on your bed and take deep, cleansing breaths. Relax until you find the place somewhere in your mind where you feel calm and relaxed. It might be a beach, a garden, a river, or anywhere you feel is "you." This is your secret place where you can go whenever you wish. After a short time you will find that you can easily slip in and out of your secret place, even at work.

A Great Exercise

Visualize your special place for a few minutes until you feel truly relaxed. Behind your place is a hill. There are boulders and rocks on the hill, representing obstacles in your way and problems to be overcome. Go up that hill and push all those boulders and rocks out of the way. Watch them roll down the hill until they disappear.

Another Great Exercise!

Visualize your secret place again until you feel relaxed. Look at the birds in the sky and notice their freedom as they circle above. Ask them to carry love and peace around the world. Feel the love and peace around you. You will soon feel guided by your intuition and will find exercises as unique as you are. When you feel ready, return to your armchair or bed.

Meditation is particularly important to women living in the modern world, so please at least try it once. We all need time out, but in a world where it is usually the woman who is looking after the children, we tend not to take enough time out for ourselves. Result? Depression, stress, anger, and resentment—none of which is good for us. When we are stressed, instead of enjoying our time with our children, we end up taking our anger out on them. Childhood is so short, isn't it worth treating yourself to ten minutes a day of relaxation and meditation?

☆ Gemstone Magick

Jewelry has been around since time began. We all love the sparkle of gemstones, but did you know just how powerful certain gemstones can be? Opposite we have listed several gemstones and how they might be beneficial to you. When looking for a new piece of jewelry, consider the list and choose a piece with a specific gemstone for you or a friend. Alternatively, carry a gemstone in your purse.

Some witches wear amber jewelry. Amber and jet have a cathartic effect by bringing into the mind the past we have buried, so that you must deal with it once and for all. These gemstones are not recommended for anyone who is suffering from depression or guilt.

STONE	USES/QUALITIES
Agate	Good for self-esteem, earthing, and energy
Amazonite	Soothes nervous system; uplifting
Amethyst	Good for healing, psychic protection, insomnia
Aventurine	Good for skin conditions; mind enhancing
Bloodstone	Soothing, calming; good for attracting money
Carnelian	Good for confidence; heals depression and pain
Citrine	Calming; regulates the urinary tract
Emerald	Strengthens memory; attracts money
Fluorite	Good for harmony and peace
Hematite	Good for strength, energy, blood purification
Jasper	Controls epilepsy
Lapis Lazuli	Good as a psychic enhancer; strengthens heart
Malachite	Good for tissue regeneration and allergies
Moonstone	Good for sterility; regulates menstrual cycle
Obsidian	Powerful healer
Onyx	Good for serenity and male prostate problems
Opal	Good for self-esteem and contentment
Peridot	Aids digestion
Quartz	Good for healing
Rose Quartz	Good for serenity and love

5 Lucky in Life Spells

✩ *Introduction*

The following spells are for luck in your life rather than for luck in love. You cannot control the feelings of another person, so you cannot perform a love spell on someone and hope to live happily ever after. On the other hand, you can use a love spell to help true love find its way to you.

What we have tried to teach you throughout this book is that YOU have control of YOUR life and of all the opportunities you've ever dreamed of. When you try out the spells and see the results, you will become more confident in yourself, which in turn will reflect in EVERY area of your life, including your love life. As you grow and work with The Craft, you will attract wonderful new opportunities into your life and this includes wonderful new people. Just be patient and it will all fall into place!

TIPS AND TALES

* * * * * * * * * *

Here are a few witchy ways to help yourself for the future:

Do not make any plans for the future when the moon is New and don't make any promises during this time either.

*

During the time when the moon goes from Full to New you should plant root vegetables, get rid of rubbish, clean the house, end bad relationships, or give up bad habits.

*

When the moon goes from New to Full, go full steam ahead with spells, hopes, and dreams, plant flowers, and start diets.

*

If you clean out your closet with the old moon, you will replace old items with new things when the New Moon comes.

*

If you wash clothes on New Year's Day, you will wash someone out of your life in the coming year.

On New Year's Eve burn all your old calendars at midnight and say: "Burn old year burn, turn New Year turn. Troubles that I burn away, never return."

☆ Endless Luck

Wouldn't it be nice to know that you could have endless luck in your life? Well, the good news is that you can by following this simple candle spell.

INGREDIENTS

* * * * * * *

One green candle

))⟨⟨

Time to visualize

The best day to start this is on a Friday. Ask the goddess to bless your candle and inscribe "Endless Luck" into it. Light the candle and look into the flame. As the flame grows higher and higher, imagine it is your luck growing. Imagine the letters L*U*C*K rising in the flames. Close your eyes and press your palms together, as if in prayer. Say six times:

"Goddess of fortune, please end my phase of bad luck. My good luck returns, my bad luck has ended. Thank you. So mote it be."

Do this spell for nine days in total and your luck will improve.

A Wishing Stone

Yes, you read that right! You can make yourself a wishing stone quite easily and bring much luck into your life. Just follow the instructions below…

If you don't have a "pet rock," seek out a large smooth stone. Paint the rune symbol *Feoh* in red on it and place it on your hearth or in a prominent place in your living room. This is the sign of prosperity. Whenever you desire a new job or money, rubbing the Wishing Stone and speaking your wish aloud will bring you whatever you wish for. Be warned though that you will weaken the stone's power if you do this too often.

INGREDIENT

* * * * * * *

A large smooth stone

Spell provided by Faolin Na Amorak.

Lucky Lady Spell

This spell has been handed down from an unknown source, but has worked many times for all who have used it. Use it when you need a little extra luck in your life. This spell is particularly good if you need luck on a specific day.

INGREDIENTS

* * * * * * *

Five sprigs of rosemary

Some green ribbon

*A small circle of paper
(about the size of a quarter)*

Take the five sprigs of rosemary and make a small doll out of them. Use the green ribbon to tie the sprigs together. It doesn't matter if you are not creative; the important thing is that you make the doll. Draw a face on the circle of paper. Make it happy (rather than sad) and add as much or as little detail as you like. Now you have your doll, give her a name—mine is called Lucky Lucy!

Once you are content with the finished result, place her in a prominent place in your kitchen, such as a shelf, or hang her by a piece of ribbon from the ceiling. Anywhere is suitable, as long as you will be able to see her. Say:

"Lucky Lucy (or whatever name you call her), I give you a home, warmth, and comfort in return for your luck and good fortune. Help me in my quest for good luck and return any bad luck to its original source. Thank you. So mote it be."

Whenever you go to the kitchen, take a moment to smile at your lucky lady. Thank her for helping you.

SUCCESS USING THIS SPELL

* * * * * * * * *

I have used this spell many times
to bring me good fortune,
particularly when I have needed
it for a specific meeting. Try it.
It's fun and it works!

☆ The Pink Candle Spell

This is one of my own personal spells and one of my all-time favorites. Use this candle spell whenever you need luck or good fortune to come quickly into your life. You may be in debt and need a helping hand, or you may want to start a class, but have no way of paying for it. Whatever it may be, the pink candle spell will help you out.

Each day for ten days you will light a pink candle in the same place in your home. Choose a place where the candle is no danger to (or in no danger from) children or animals. Concentrate and visualize what you want the candle to provide. When you are happy with your choice, light the candle and say:

"This pink candle represents my growth. This pink candle is my link to a better future for me. This pink candle will show me the way. This pink candle will light my dark path. Thank you. So mote it be."

Take a moment to reflect on what you have said and feel the happiness you would feel if someone could guarantee your wish and make your dreams come true. Allow the candle to burn down. Repeat this ritual for ten days. Your wish will soon be granted!

Tips
• If you don't have pink candles, white ones will do.
• For a lovely aroma, rub rose oil onto each candle.
Spell provided by Midia Star.

INGREDIENTS

* * * * * * *

Ten pink candles

SUCCESS USING THIS SPELL

* * * * * * * * * * *

I designed this spell myself because of the simple fact that I didn't have any other color candles in the house! The results were quick and amazing. When a coworker broke down in tears because she couldn't afford the money to pay a bill, I offered her the pink candle spell. She tried it and by the third day of using it, she received an unexpected check in the mail. It met her needs and she had some money left over to treat herself!

☆ *Lucky in Love Spell* ♡

This isn't a love spell as such. We don't believe that you can influence another person's love in any way, shape, or form. However, that shouldn't stop you from helping yourself when you've had a run of bad luck in the love department! Some women wonder why they go from one bad relationship to the next, or why they always fall for Mr. Wrong, never Mr. Right. Some women fall into abusive relationships again and again. Why? It has to do with the power of attraction and your self-worth. If you think that you don't deserve any better than an abusive relationship, then that is what you are going to get, time and time again. This spell is about YOU, not him. Always remember the Sevenfold Law. If someone has hurt you in the past, they WILL get their comeuppance, but you don't have to suffer a horrible relationship; you can have a happy love life. You deserve it, don't you?

INGREDIENTS

* * * * * * *

An Action Figure doll

((((«

Cardamom or rosemary

You may feel foolish doing this, but believe me it works! First of all trace the outline of your Action Figure on an 8½" x 11" (21 cm x 28 cm) piece of paper. Next, draw as many arrows as you like going from the figure to within about an inch (2 cm) of the edge of the paper. Now imagine carefully what your ideal partner would be like. Would he be romantic and bring you flowers every day? Would he surprise you with weekend trips? Or perhaps you like a rough and ready man, with a soft heart? What does he do for a job? Maybe he's a man about town? A builder? A serviceman? Whatever your ideal man is like, write

it down—even the color of his eyes and hair. Be specific in what you want from your ideal man. You might not want him in your life 24 hours a day and might want to see him only on weekends. If so, write this down, too. It's nice to have a partner, but we women do like our own space, too!

On the back of the paper, write down what it is you DON'T want—maybe you don't want him to snore? Maybe you've been in a bad relationship before. You don't want another one like that, do you? Whatever you don't want, jot it down.

Next, take your Action Figure and dress him in the type of clothes your ideal man would wear. It might be difficult to find the right type of clothing, but, if all else fails, make something that you like. Once you are happy with how he looks, sprinkle your chosen herbs on top of your ideal man and say:

"This figure represents my ideal man—the man who will come into my life and love me for who I am. My ideal man will treat me well and give me the happiness that I deserve. Thank you. So mote it be."

Keep the Action Figure next to your bed. The most important part of this spell is your belief that you will find not only Mr. Right but also your ideal man. If you really believe that you will find him, then sure enough, he will soon enter your life.

Spell provided by Midia Star.

When Spells Don't Work

There are times in every witch's life when a certain spell just won't work. Don't panic if this happens. There can be many reasons why a request isn't being met. It could be that you are doing it at the wrong time of the month. Check what phase the moon is in. It could be that you are doing a spell for the benefit of another person and not truly for yourself. If this is the case, then it will never work. You can't fool your subconscious! For example, if you are doing a spell to get a promotion because your partner thinks it will be good for you, but you really yearn to leave and open your own business, then no amount of Magick is going to get you that promotion, because it's not YOUR desire. If it does work you are not going to be happy with the results.

Another reason is that you might have fallen into the trap of doing spells just for the sheer fun of it, to show off to others, or to "test" Magick. Such spells won't work!

Sometimes, the time is just not right. For example, if you do the Lucky in Love Spell, but you are not really ready to start a new relationship, it won't work because you might still be holding resentment, or be hurting in some way. If you find that this is the case and a particular spell hasn't worked for you, wait 28 days and try again. Twenty-eight days is the time it takes for the moon to return to its original position, not 30 or 31 as the calendar states.

6

A Witch's Garden

☆ A Witch's Garden

A witch's garden is full of wonderful herbs, which she can use in a number of ways such as for cooking, medicines, and, of course, in spells. Herbs grow best in poor, stony, well-drained soil, and invasive herbs such as mint should be grown in pots, otherwise they will take over your garden! You must also remember to nip the flowers from invasive herbs, otherwise bees will cross-pollinate and you will end up with your spearmint, apple-mint, and cloves all tasting the same.

Herbs can be used to make wonderful teas, for bathing wounds, and even for diaper rash—calendula and thyme are excellent for this purpose. For cleansing and purifying and for banishing spells, use basil water, either in a ritual or around the house.

Most women today are familiar with aromatherapy, but just how many of us recognize its links with The Craft? Ylang-ylang and yarrow make a wonderful aphrodisiac, as will a bowl of foxglove leaves on the bedside table. You don't need to spend a fortune on moisturizer either. If you blend some glycerin and rosewater together you will achieve the same, if not better, results as any of the top brand moisturizers on the market today. Use rosewater on its own as a skin toner. And lavender water is a wonderful alternative freshener for bed linen.

Fill your house with the flowers you love and you'll soon see a difference in the whole atmosphere.

The only "don't" is try not to use anything green indoors. So green paint, carpets, and curtains are a no-no. Green is the color of nature and belongs outdoors. It is said to be unlucky to paint the inside of your house in green. However, you can use green from natural sources, so by all means have as many green plants, flowers, vegetables, and fruits as you like in your house.

Maybe you have a formal herb garden with a sundial in the middle or are fortunate enough to have a cottage garden, or maybe you have a small patio garden or even a small balcony—whatever your garden type, the following plants are traditional choices for inclusion in the witch's garden:

* Foxgloves and lemon balm to attract bees. Slugs won't eat foxgloves—or any plants with scented leaves. (NB: Never grow edible herbs near foxgloves.)
* Garlic to keep greenfly away.
* Bay to protect your home.
* Catnip (planted near the step) to bring you money.
* Lavender and basil to give you psychic protection.
* Parsley (sown on a Good Friday to ensure it grows well).
* Fennel for fennel tea—a slimming aid.
* Calendula for its color and healing properties—and to please the goddess.
* Sweet peas, Sweet Williams, night-scented stock, and anything that smells delicious.
* Mixed flowers—these are easy to sow and are loved by all!

Nature's Bounty

Food, moisturizers, and medicine are all part of nature's generous bounty, as you will discover with a little research and experimentation. Here are a few examples of what's on offer in your garden and the natural world in general. You will soon discover that most beauty products you can buy in a department store are available to you from natural sources. And you will save a fortune on cosmetics, medicine, and food!

☆ Hedgerow Jam

Hedgerow jam can be made in exactly the same way that you make jam using store-bought fruit, but by using rose hips, blackberries, sloes and crab apples or wild plums instead, you will have a truly natural jam that will enrich the blood and keep colds at bay. Sloes and elderberries give jam a slightly "dry" flavor, rather like dry wine.

☆ Horse Chestnuts

If you think the old horse chestnut tree's fruits are just for the kids, think again! If you can persuade the kids to give you two pounds (a kilo) of horse chestnuts, you can make a wonderful bath lotion. Simply chop the chestnuts up and boil them in water for twenty minutes. Strain them and, when the remaining mixture has cooled, pour it into screw-top jars, adding a little gin to preserve it. Next time you take a bath, add a little of the mixture to your bathwater. Horse chestnut leaves also make wonderful soft soap leaves. Try washing your face with one and see!

Provided by Faolin Na Amorak.

ELDER COUGH MEDICINE

If you are lucky, you will find elder in your garden. Elder is sacred to the ancient one (The Crone) and we cannot stress enough the respect you must give to her. Always ask permission when picking the flowers or fruit. For a great cough syrup, you will need:

1 lb (450 g) elderberries

1 lb (450 g) ripe rose hips

5 or 6 cloves

1 lb (450 g) dark soft sugar

Wash the fruit and place it in a large ovenproof basin. Cover the basin and place it in a warm oven to "juice." When you have a warm juice, blend the fruit with an electric blender and put it in a pan with the cloves. Add the sugar, bring to a boil, and simmer until you have a syrup. Strain the syrup through an old, clean tea towel. Bottle when cooled.

This is one of the best cough medicines ever! Take one teaspoonful as necessary.

7 Being Your Own Witch

☆ *Introduction*

As you work through the spells we have provided in this book, you will soon become more confident that you can have anything you want by simply applying some modern Magick to your life. Some witchcraft books state that you must do this and must do that—we don't. So long as you believe that a certain ritual WILL work for you, you will succeed.

Other people's spells don't always work. There are some spells that just don't work for you, no matter how hard you try. If you don't feel comfortable with a particular spell, then adapt it to your own requirements. If, for example, you don't have the exact ingredients specified in a particular spell, then improvise. You will find that, because you have added your own personal touch, the spell will be more powerful.

Making your own spells is easy. Just try to follow the suggestions about moon phases, colors, days, and herbs that we have given you in this book and you can make up your own spells. For example, do so with the Action Figure spell. You may well have a husband or a partner and do not require a new man in your life, but instead require a change in your partner's attitude toward you. If this is the case, then adapt the spell to your own needs. Make up words that apply to your circumstances. The reason we use rhyming words is because they are easier to say and remember, particularly if a spell requires you to repeat the words over a number of days.

The mind is the most powerful tool you will ever have and it is always open to suggestion. The only reason we don't have what we want in life is because we limit ourselves. Instead of granting ourselves the ability to achieve anything, we let ourselves give in to doubt and limitations. Always remember, a thought is just a thought. It's only when we believe a negative thought that we allow it to limit us and our ability to get what we want out of life.

We're not here on Earth for that long. Free the little witch in you and get everything you want out of your life!

Appreciating the Magick ✳

We hope you enjoyed reading this book as much as we have
enjoyed writing it. As you have seen, Magick is not necessarily
about dedicating your life to the religion of Wicca. Any woman
can apply these practices to her life, regardless of what religion
she has been brought up in or believes in now. The main
emphasis is on the belief that you CAN have the life you want.

The art of The Craft demonstrates not only how to attain the results
you want out of life, but also the enjoyment of what you already have in
your life now. In the modern society that we live in, we are encouraged
to focus on what we *don't* have, rather than what we *do* have. We are
encouraged to focus on the fact that we don't have the top of the line
BMW parked in the garage, rather than on the fact that some people
don't even have the ability to drive a car, be it an old jalopy or a brand
new status car.

We forget that for most of us our children are safe, happy, and
healthy, while for others this is not so. And when the household bills
mount up, we allow ourselves to feel miserable about having to pay
them, rather than realizing how lucky we are to have a nice warm home.

There's nothing more uplifting than to spend some time thinking
about just how lucky we really are to be where we are, regardless of
circumstances. This "time-out" will make you realize that things are not
as bad as you think and will also remind you that you can get through
anything and still come out smiling. Try the following exercise and see!

Thankful Exercise

There are times in every woman's life when everything looks bleak and she wonders if it's all worth it. Whenever you feel like this, take a pad of notepaper and write on it all the positive things you do have. The rule is that you are not allowed to dwell on the things you don't have in your life right now, because if you follow the information in this book you will have them at some point in your future.

Marianne's Thankful Exercise Example

Marianne is a 30-year-old mother of two who has just come out of an abusive relationship. She is living with her sister temporarily, in a small, overcrowded apartment. She doesn't work (because one child is still at home) and she doesn't have much money.

    Instead of focusing on what she doesn't have, Marianne writes down what she does have:

✳ *I have two wonderful, healthy children I have brought up single-handedly. I am an excellent mother and role model to them both.*

✳ *I have been strong enough to overcome my fears and leave an abusive relationship.*

✳ *I am lucky to have a roof over my head instead of being out on the street.*

✳ *I am able to live on a budget and invent ideas for economic meals.*

✳ *I am here for my children, day or night.*

Doesn't that sound better than moaning and groaning on about what she doesn't have? As soon as we look at what we do have, rather than what our life lacks, our confidence grows. We really should give ourselves more credit for the things that we experience and cope with in life. Each obstacle we come across, be it finding the money to pay for a school trip, or getting through a bereavement, makes us stronger and more confident women. When you do the "Thankful Exercise," you will find that you suddenly start thinking, "I'm not so bad after all" and "If I survived that, I can do anything!"

Whenever you get depressed about things, do this exercise and remind yourself of what you have to be thankful for. You will begin to feel more positive about yourself, which is the frame of mind required to perform all Magick.

Remember, a thought is just a thought. If it's a negative thought, it can just as easily be changed to a positive thought. No one except you owns your thoughts and it is only you who can change them. So, that negative thought about your partner dumping you could easily be turned into a positive thought, if you allow it. Yes, he might have been great in bed, but could you see yourself with him twenty years from now? Even if you shout "Yes, I could!" then remember, two people who are meant to be together will stay together despite everything. Make sure that the next one you pick won't turn out to be some guy who doesn't truly want to be with you. The same thing applies to losing your job. You can dwell on the fact that you have no money and no career and spend the next week crying your eyes out. Or you can delight in the fact that you now have more time to spend with the children, take up that art class that is free to unemployed people, be creative, and do what you want to do with your life. Remember, we live in a universe where all our NEEDS are met, even though it might look bleak at the moment.

Until we meet again, make a promise to yourself to have the most wonderful life ever, because you're worth it and it's only you who can make it happen. So free the little witch in you!

Appendix:
Moon Phases

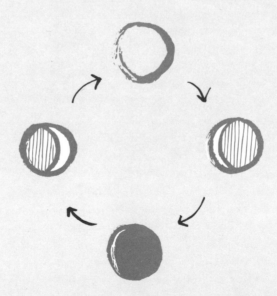

Moon phases: The following pages offer an easy reference to what phase the moon is in for the years 2004–2011. It is not imperative to do a spell on a particular night when the moon is in a particular phase, but it will give more power to your spell if you do (see page 11).

2004

MONTH/PHASE	Waxing Moon	Full Moon	Waning Moon	New Moon
January	21	28	6	13
February	20	27	4	12
March	22	28	6	14
April	20	27	4	12
May	19	26	4	12
June	18	24	3	10
July	17	24	2	10
August	15	22	1 & 31	8
September	13	21	29	7
October	13	21	29	6
November	11	20	27	4
December	11	19	27	4

2005

MONTH/PHASE	Waxing Moon	Full Moon	Waning Moon	New Moon
January	17	25	3	10
February	15	24	2	8
March	17	25	3	10
April	16	24	2	8
May	16	23	1 & 30	8
June	15	22	28	6
July	14	21	28	6
August	13	19	26	5
September	11	18	25	3
October	10	17	25	3
November	9	16	23	2
December	8	15	23	1 & 31

2006

MONTH/PHASE	Waxing Moon	Full Moon	Waning Moon	New Moon
January	6	14	22	29
February	5	13	21	28
March	6	14	22	29
April	5	13	21	27
May	5	13	20	27
June	3	11	18	25
July	3	11	17	25
August	2 & 31	9	16	23
September	30	7	14	22
October	29	7	14	22
November	28	5	12	20
December	27	5	12	20

2007

MONTH/PHASE	Waxing Moon	Full Moon	Waning Moon	New Moon
January	25	3	11	19
February	24	2	10	17
March	25	3	12	19
April	24	2	10	17
May	23	2	10	16
June	22	1 & 30	8	15
July	22	30	7	14
August	20	28	5	12
September	19	26	4	11
October	19	26	3	11
November	17	24	1	9
December	17	24	1 & 31	9

2008

MONTH/PHASE	Waxing Moon	Full Moon	Waning Moon	New Moon
January	15	22	30	8
February	14	21	29	7
March	14	21	29	7
April	12	20	28	6
May	12	20	28	5
June	10	18	26	3
July	10	18	25	3
August	8	16	24	1 & 30
September	7	15	22	29
October	7	14	21	28
November	6	13	19	27
December	5	12	19	27

2009

MONTH/PHASE	Waxing Moon	Full Moon	Waning Moon	New Moon
January	4	11	18	26
February	2	9	16	25
March	4	11	18	26
April	2	9	17	25
May	1 & 31	9	17	24
June	29	7	15	22
July	28	7	15	22
August	27	6	13	20
September	26	4	12	18
October	26	4	11	18
November	24	2	9	16
December	24	2	9	16

2010

MONTH/PHASE	Waxing Moon	Full Moon	Waning Moon	New Moon
January	23	30	7	15
February	22	28	5	14
March	23	30	7	15
April	21	28	6	14
May	20	27	6	14
June	19	26	4	12
July	18	26	4	11
August	16	24	3	10
September	15	23	1	8
October	14	23	1 & 30	7
November	13	21	28	6
December	13	21	28	5

2011

MONTH/PHASE	Waxing Moon	Full Moon	Waning Moon	New Moon
January	12	19	26	4
February	11	18	24	3
March	12	19	26	4
April	11	18	25	3
May	10	17	24	3
June	9	15	23	1
July	8	15	23	1
August	6	13	21	29
September	4	12	20	27
October	4	12	20	26
November	2	10	18	25
December	2	10	18	24

✩ Index

* * * * * * * * * * * * * * * * * * *